**ALL
ABOUT**

Animals
and
Their Young

Written and illustrated by

Robert M. McClung

allabout
books

**RANDOM
HOUSE
NEW YORK**

For My Sons

Contents

Contents

1. All Kinds of Young

Everyone feels good when spring comes and the cold dark days of winter fade away. A stirring of new life comes over the land. The air is warmer and the sky brighter. Every day the sun rises earlier than it did the day before and sets later. The branches of trees start to show green or red or yellow at their tips. You can see a change every day. You can smell it in the blossoms and hear it in the returning birds. Most of all, you can *feel* it everywhere.

All About Animals and Their Young

In the spring all kinds of animals are more active than usual. Many of them are getting ready to have their families. On all sides you can hear the cheery song of the robin, the soft call of the bluebird, or the loud clear whistle of the redwing. These are male birds, busily staking out nesting territories. Far overhead, wild geese honk as they fly in V-formation to their nesting grounds farther north.

In the ponds and marsh areas, frogs and toads have wakened from their winter sleep and are trilling to each other. Many fish are preparing underwater nests or are swimming upstream to lay their eggs. Insects are laying their eggs in all sorts of places.

Furred animals are busy taking care of their young ones too. Cottontail rabbits nurse their offspring in snug hidden nests in the fields. Baby squirrels peer out of leafy shelters high in the treetops and blink at the bright world outside. Deep in the shady woods a doe nuzzles her spotted fawn.

Although some animals bear young at any time, lots of them have their families at a definite season. Spring is one of the best times in all the year for having a family. The weather is mild, the days are long, and there is usually an abundance of food.

In the spring the peepers trill in marsh and pond areas.

How the Simplest Animals Reproduce

If you scoop up a cupful of water from a pond in the spring and examine it with a magnifying glass or microscope, you may see all kinds of tiny strange creatures. Each consists of only one cell. Many of them are too small to be seen with the naked eye. They come in all sorts of different shapes. Most of them are almost transparent. They are called *protozoans*, which means "first animals."

Some of them look like tiny blobs of jelly, about one-hundredth of an inch across. They move by changing shape, putting out arms of their body material, or protoplasm, and flowing in that direction. These are amoebas. They reproduce by the simple method of splitting in half. Each half is a smaller duplicate of the individual from which it split. This method of reproduction is called *fission*.

Besides the amoeba, there are larger sausage-shaped protozoans in the cup which swim rapidly through the water. These are *paramecia*. Each paramecium divides by fission too. It splits crossways, at its middle, as often as once or twice a day.

Sometimes two paramecia come together side by side. The cell wall of each breaks down, and internal

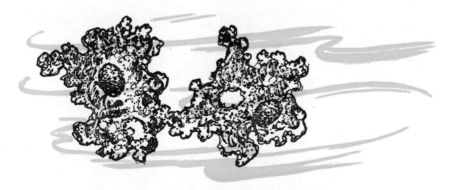

With a microscope we can see an amoeba splitting in half. The dark circles are nuclei.

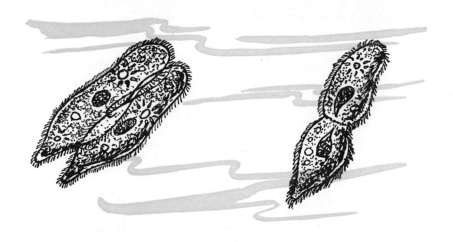

Two paramecia (left) come together to exchange internal material. A single paramecium (right) divides into two.

material flows between the two individuals. Each gives portions of its nucleus or life center to the other. This exchange puts new life into each animal. Now it has new vigor with which to go about reproduction by splitting.

In the same cup of water with the protozoans, you may see much larger creatures that have trunklike bodies topped by a number of waving limbs or tentacles. These are hydras. Each one is from an eighth to three-quarters of an inch long. It clings to the side of the cup or to a water weed and looks almost like a plant itself.

Hydras have several different ways of reproducing. One of them is similar to the way many plants reproduce. A tiny new hydra grows out of the main trunk of the parent, just as a branch grows out from the trunk of the tree. Eventually the young hydra breaks off and goes its own way. This method of reproduction is called budding. Sponges and corals reproduce by budding too.

In some cases a complete new animal will grow from a part. This is true of a starfish. If one arm and part of the center are broken off, a whole new starfish will grow from this portion. If a flatworm is cut in two, each part grows into a complete new worm.

The Earthworm, the Aphid and the Jellyfish

Most animals that we are familiar with reproduce sexually. That is, each species has two different sexes, male and female. The female animal produces special cells, called ova or eggs. The male produces cells called sperms. In sexual reproduction the sperm from a male animal joins the egg cell of a female animal. These two cells together form what we call a fertilized egg. The fertilized egg promptly begins to divide and develop. Eventually it becomes a baby animal of that species.

In a few cases, one animal can develop both eggs

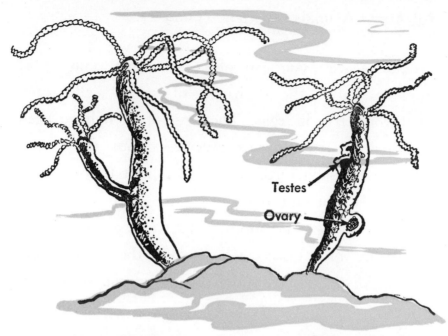

Testes

Ovary

The hydra at the left is reproducing by budding. The other
(right) contains both egg and sperm cells for reproduction.

and sperm cells. This is the case with the hydra, which
can reproduce sexually as well as by budding. Egg
cells develop in one swelling of its trunk, and sperm
cells in another. The sperms are cast into the water
and may fertilize the eggs on the same trunk, or the
eggs of another hydra.

Earthworms have both egg and sperm cells too.
When egg-laying time approaches, two earthworms
come out of their burrows and lie side by side, ex-
changing sperm cells. If you take a flashlight and go
out in the lawn some night in late spring when the

ground is wet, you can often see them doing this. Sometime after the exchange of sperm cells, each earthworm lays its eggs. The eggs of each have been fertilized by the sperms received from the other. Thus each young earthworm will inherit traits of two individuals, not just one.

Aphids show still another way of having young. These are tiny insects which suck the juices from plants. All the aphids which appear in the spring are

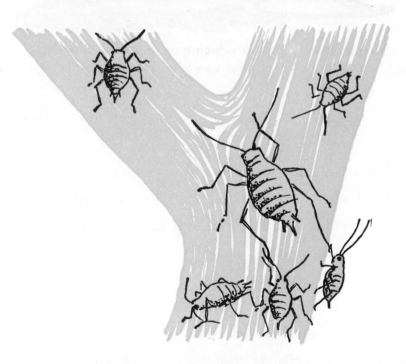

Tiny female aphids, born in the spring, suck the juices from plants with their mother.

8

females which soon start bearing live young. There are no male aphids around to fertilize the females' eggs, but the eggs develop anyway—into females just like their mother. This all-female society goes on generation after generation all summer long.

In the autumn a generation finally appears which includes both males and females. These mate, and the females lay fertile eggs. The next spring the eggs hatch into females, and the pattern starts all over again.

Some animals have a generation of sexual individuals and then one that is non-sexual. Each looks quite different from the other. This is the case with many jellyfish. *Aurelia* is a free-swimming saucer-like jellyfish which we sometimes see when we are in swimming. It is the sexual form of the species, called a medusa. At the proper time the male medusa discharges his sperm cells into the water. Some are taken by water currents into the female's body cavity where they fertilize her eggs. The eggs develop within the female until they are disgorged as free-swimming larvae which look quite different from the adult medusas. The larvae settle on the bottom and grow into branched animals called polyps. The polyps

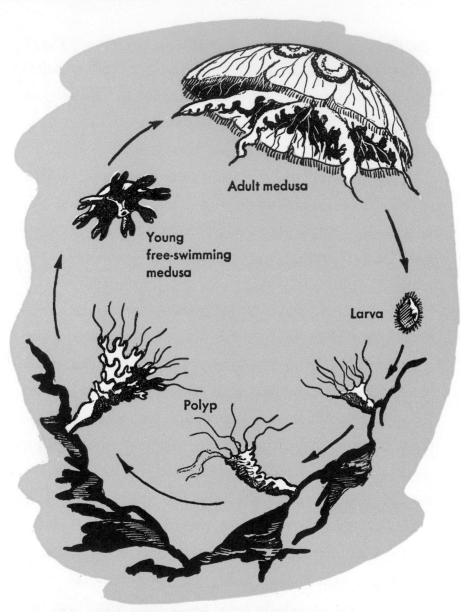

Adult medusa

Young
free-swimming
medusa

Larva

Polyp

The Aurelia jellyfish passes through the four stages of
development shown above.

are the non-sexual generation of the jellyfish. Like the hydra they reproduce by budding off other polyps. At a certain time every year each polyp develops what look like flat discs. These break away, one by one, and become free-swimming individuals. Each is a small medusa which grows and becomes an adult male or female *Aurelia* like the one we started with.

As you can see, nature has worked out many different methods for having young.

How Many Young?

Some animals have tremendous numbers of young at one time. The codfish can lay three or four million eggs each season, while an oyster can produce nine million eggs, and a sea urchin twenty million. The sea hare, a kind of marine snail, tops all these. It can lay eggs at the rate of 40,000 or so a minute—and keep that up day in and day out for weeks. It was once estimated that a pair had laid 478 million eggs in a little over four months.

All of these champion egg-layers are water animals. At the rate they lay eggs, you would think that the ocean would be full of codfish, oysters, sea urchins and sea hares. But not at all. The eggs and young of these animals face so many dangers that few grow up. The mother has to produce thousands of eggs for a few to survive.

Mammals and birds never have such spectacular numbers of young. They do not need to, for they give their young more care and protection. Although an elephant may live seventy years or more, it usually has only four or five babies in a lifetime. The whale has no more than one every two years. Animals like these are so big and powerful that they have few enemies.

The tiny field mouse is very different. In its life-time it probably is able to produce more young than any other mammal. One scientist estimated that under ideal conditions a pair of field mice could have seven-teen litters in one year, with four to nine in each litter. That means 68 to 153 babies a year. But field mice have many enemies—weasels, foxes, hawks, owls, snakes and many more. They have to produce lots of babies for a few to survive.

Some animals almost always have the same number of young in each clutch or litter. The king penguin, the California condor, and the puffin all brood only

The ruby-throated hummingbird usually has a family of two.

one egg at a time. The hummingbird almost invariably lays two eggs, and the killdeer four.

Many of the larger mammals ordinarily have only one young at a time. This is the case with elephants and hippopotamuses, horses and cows, monkeys and great apes. It is the case with human beings too. Human twins come along about once in every eighty-four births. Triplets occur only once in 7,056 cases, which is eighty-four times eighty-four. And human quadruplets and quintuplets are so rare they get written up in all the newspapers.

The nine-banded armadillo, on the other hand, always has four young at a time, and these are always of the same sex. That is because the four individuals started life as a single fertilized egg which split into four separate parts. Each of these developed into an individual animal. The baby armadillos are identical quadruplets.

Like Father, Like Son?

Often animal babies are so different from their parents that they are not recognizable as the same species. This is especially true of insects.

I shall never forget finding a big green caterpillar when I was a boy. It was three inches long, thicker around than my thumb, and well decorated with red spots. My granddad called it a leaf-eater. I kept it to see what it would do. Soon the caterpillar spun a cocoon around itself, and all winter long it lay on a shelf in my bedroom.

The next spring the cocoon hatched, and out came a strange creature with a white furry body and yellow

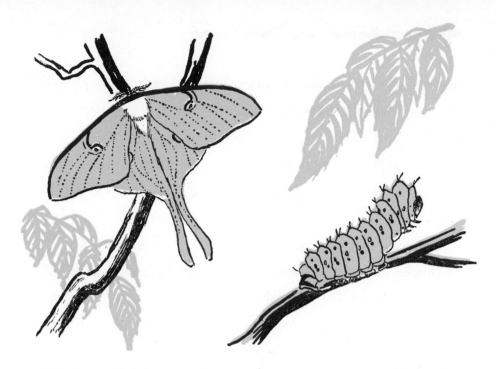

The beautiful luna moth comes from a big green caterpillar.

plumed antennae. Damp pads jutted out of its back. Soon they became wide green wings, edged with purple. Each hind wing narrowed into a long trailing tail. The crawling leaf-eater had become a beautiful luna moth.

Many insects change just as dramatically as this during their development. Flies lay eggs which hatch into white, legless maggots or larvae. These eat and grow and then go through a resting or pupal period before becoming winged adults. The larvae of dragonflies are wingless, crawling creatures which live in the water and breathe by means of gills. Later they come out of the water and become swift, flashing dragonflies.

This great change which many insects go through is called *metamorphosis* which means "to change form."

Besides insects, many other kinds of invertebrates (animals without backbones) go through similar changes. Starfish and shellfish, for example, look completely different from their own free-swimming larvae.

Among the vertebrates (animals with backbones), the newborn young are often quite different from the parents. Frogs and toads start life as polliwogs or tadpoles. They go through a metamorphosis too. You can watch the whole transformation if you gather several strings of toad eggs from a pond in April or May. When the tiny toad tadpole hatches, it has no legs. It swims by wiggling its tail back and forth. It has branched gills for breathing and a small oval mouth.

But day by day, changes take place. The branched outside gills are replaced by gills hidden inside the body. Tiny buds appear on either side of the tail.

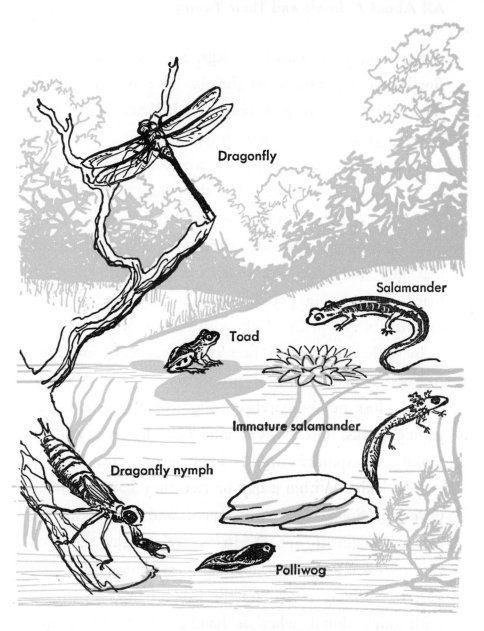

The larvae of dragonflies, toads and salamanders all live in water. After metamorphosis they leave the water.

These soon grow into hind legs. Forelegs appear, and finally the tail begins to shrink. The round tadpole head changes into a knobby toad head. The small mouth gradually widens into a gaping opening. Nostrils appear. In about six weeks the tadpole has changed into a tiny toad, less than half an inch long.

Young reptiles, on the other hand, usually look quite like their parents, although their color and markings may be different. One baby snake—the black racer—has a gay black and tan pattern, while its parents are plain black with white bellies.

In birds the contrast between the young and their parents is mainly one of proportions and outer covering. Most newly hatched songbirds have enormous gaping beaks, closed eyes and bald heads that nod shakily on spindly necks. They grow and develop very quickly. Within a day or two they have a downy covering. Soon their eyes open, and the first true feathers begin to sprout. In several weeks they are ready to leave the nest looking very much like their parents. A baby chick, on the other hand, is covered with thick down when it hatches. It needs a long time to grow adult feathers and the comb and wattles of the hen or rooster.

Newborn mammal babies usually look like the father and mother, just as with human infants. But sometimes you have to look carefully to see the resemblance. A baby black bear, for instance, is naked at birth and no bigger than a rat. Its eyes are closed, and its crinkly, folded ears are hugged tight against its head. Altogether it is a most unbear-like animal! Yet if you look closely, you can see it has typically bear-shaped feet, the bearlike muzzle, and the stubby bear tail.

The young of marsupials, or pouched animals—like the opossum and kangaroo—are so tiny and undeveloped at birth that they have practically no resemblance to their parents at all.

Many young mammals have a covering of fur or wool very different from their parents' fur. Some newborn seals have white woolly coats which are soon shed and replaced by smooth dark or spotted hair like their parents'. Baby South American tapirs have coats striped with white while the parents are plain brown. The fawns of most deer are spotted. But by fall of their first year the spots have usually disappeared, and both sexes look like small editions of their mother. The next year the male fawn grows

Sometimes the white-tailed deer fawn is almost invisible.

spike antlers. Each year thereafter he gets larger and more spreading antlers until he reaches his prime. Then at last it can be said that he looks just like his father.

What's in a Name?

When we talk about animals, we use different names to distinguish between young animals and their parents. The young of cattle are calves, and the young of horses are foals or colts. Sheep have lambs, deer have fawns, dogs have puppies and lions have cubs.

Sometimes we use different names for each parent animal too. Male and female cattle are bulls and cows. Horses are stallions and mares, sheep are rams and ewes, and deer are bucks and does. When we speak of nesting birds, the adult male is generally called the cock and the female the hen. The young are called nestlings or fledglings. Adult chickens are roosters and hens, and their offspring are chicks. A gander and goose have goslings.

With a few animals we even have different names to indicate different stages in the development of the young. A buck and doe are the parents of a fawn. After its first year the fawn becomes a yearling. If it is a male, it may be called a spike or button buck. Newly hatched chicks grow into poults. Then they become pullets if they are young hens and cockerels if young roosters.

Sportsmen have specialized names for different stages in the development of the Atlantic salmon. When it first hatches from the egg and still has an unabsorbed yolk sac, it is called an alevin. After it loses its yolk sac it becomes a fry or samlet, which

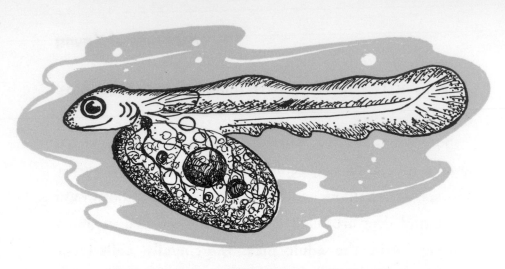

Here you see a salmon alevin with its yolk sac.

grows into a spotted minnow known as a parr. At a year or so of age when it goes to sea and changes to a silver color, it is called a smolt. Salmon that return to fresh water to breed when they are two years old are called grilse. Those which first return when they are three or four years old are known simply as salmon. The few salmon which survive to return to the ocean and then come back to the river to breed a second time, are called kelts.

The young of animals which undergo a metamorphosis between birth and adulthood are generally called larvae. Larval butterflies and moths are known as caterpillars. The larvae of flies are maggots, and the larvae of beetles are grubs. The aquatic larvae of such insects as dragonflies and May flies are known as nymphs or naiads. Larval mosquitoes are commonly called wrigglers.

This name calling can get even more complicated if we consider hybrids, which are the offspring of two closely related but different species of animals. A mule is a hybrid. It has a female horse or mare for its mother, and a male donkey or jack for its father. As with practically all hybrid animals, the mule is sterile and cannot have young of its own.

Zoo men have had to invent names for some kinds of hybrid animals. The offspring of a lion and tiger is called a "liger" if the lion is its father. If a tiger is the father, the young animal is known as a "tiglon" or "tigon." These, as you can see, are merely combinations of the words "lion" and "tiger," and are used strictly for convenience.

2. Eggs, Eggs, Eggs

Everyone knows what a bird egg is like. But few people have seen the egg of a dog or a cat, an elephant or a whale. Yet each of these animals starts as an egg too.

In many animals the eggs develop inside the mother's body where they cannot be seen. They are so small to begin with that they could hardly be seen anyway. For example, the human egg is a tiny round blob of living material only 1/166 of an inch in diameter.

It weighs about one ten-millionth of a pound. Yet from such a small beginning comes a human being. An eighty-foot whale and a four-ton elephant develop from eggs almost as small.

Why is the egg of a bird so much bigger? The answer is very simple. The bird lays its egg. Thus the embryo in the egg develops outside the mother's body. The egg must have a store of food to nourish the growing embryo and a shell to protect it. Mammal embryos, which develop inside the mother's body, get their food and protection directly from her.

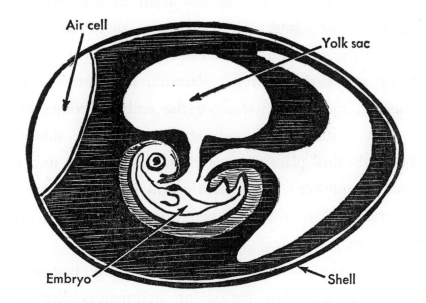

This diagram of a bird's egg shows the embryo developing inside the shell.

All About Animals and Their Young

Animals which lay their eggs are called *oviparous* animals. This word means "to bring forth eggs." All birds are oviparous. So are most insects and other invertebrates, as well as many fish, amphibians and reptiles.

Animals whose eggs develop inside the mother's body are called *viviparous*. This means "bringing forth live young." These eggs derive food from the mother. The young are born alive.

Most mammals are viviparous. When the mammal egg is fertilized, it travels down its mother's egg channel or oviduct and imbeds itself in the lining of her uterus or womb. There it begins to develop.

Soon the egg and the uterus together form a wonderful structure called the placenta. By means of the placenta, the blood stream of the embryo comes into contact with the blood stream of the mother. Through this placenta it receives food and oxygen from its mother's blood stream and gets rid of waste materials. When the baby mammal has reached a certain stage of development, it is born.

The period of development within the mother is called the gestation period or pregnancy. For the opossum it is only twelve days. For an elephant it is nearly two years. The gestation period of the house mouse is just nineteen days while that of the domestic cat is about two months. A baby lion or tiger takes slightly over three months to develop within the mother. A sheep takes five months, a zebra twelve, a giraffe fourteen, a rhinoceros seventeen.

With the human baby the gestation period is usually nine months. A human baby, however, may be born as early as six months after pregnancy begins and still survive. Such a baby is called a premature

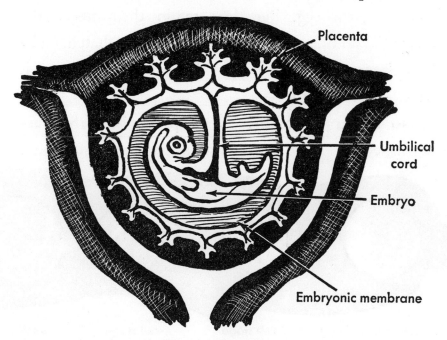

Placenta

Umbilical cord

Embryo

Embryonic membrane

Surrounded by the placenta, the mammal embryo develops inside the shell.

baby. It is placed in an incubator which provides the heat and oxygen it would have had in the mother's body.

Most animals either lay eggs that develop externally, as birds do, or give birth to young which have been nourished inside the mother's body, as mammals do.

In between, however, there are all sorts of variations. Certain insects, fish, amphibians and reptiles produce eggs with a stored-in food supply and shell like the bird egg. But they retain them inside the mother's body until they are ready to hatch. The horned lizard or toad of our Western desert areas is an example of this type.

No matter where they develop, or how they are nourished, all eggs have the same basic structure.

Single fertilized egg   2-cell stage   4-cell stage   8-cell stage

Here you see the development of a toad egg, generally typical of all egg development.

They go through the same general stages of development.

This can be observed most easily with newly laid frog or toad eggs. Within hours after the egg has been laid, it splits in two, much as the simple amoeba does. Soon each of these halves splits again, and there are four cells. Then the four split into eight cells, the eight into sixteen, the sixteen into thirty-two, and so on. Eventually there are enough cells to form a sphere like a hollow ball made up of individual cells.

Next, an indentation appears at one side of the ball, as though it had been pushed in. Here a layer of cells starts to grow inward. The developing frog or toad embryo now consists of two cell layers, one outside and one inside. Between these two a third layer develops rapidly. All of the many organs and

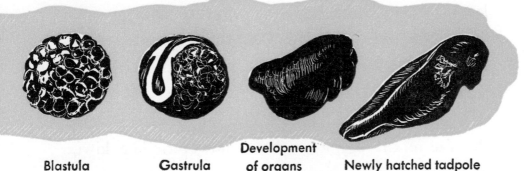

| Blastula | Gastrula | Development of organs | Newly hatched tadpole |

The blastula is the hollow-ball stage. In the gastrula stage the cells start to grow inward.

tissues of the tadpole will develop from these three layers of cells.

Soon a head forms and a tail and gills. Then the various internal organs start to form. This general sequence of events happens with every kind of egg-producing animal.

All Sizes, Shapes and Colors

Birds and reptiles have the largest eggs of any animals. Those of fish and amphibians are usually small while the eggs of many invertebrates and mammals are microscopic in size. The ostrich egg is the largest: seven inches long and five inches in diameter. It is large enough to make an omelet for a couple of dozen people. Several species of West Indian hummingbirds lay the smallest bird eggs—each only about a quarter of an inch long. This is not surprising because hummingbirds are the smallest living birds, and the ostrich is the largest.

The size of the adult bird does not always govern the size of the egg it produces, however. The kiwi, a strange flightless bird from New Zealand, is about the size of a chicken. It lays an egg which is close to

The egg of the kiwi may weigh one fourth as much as the kiwi.

five inches long and weighs nearly a pound—a fifth of the weight of the bird that laid it.

Eggs come in all sorts of shapes too. Most bird eggs are oval with one end more pointed than the other. Reptile eggs are usually round or oblong and are tapered alike at both ends. Fish eggs are usually round too. Insect eggs, however, come in almost any shape you can imagine. Some are round. Some are oval. Others may be cone-shaped, pear-shaped, bell-

31

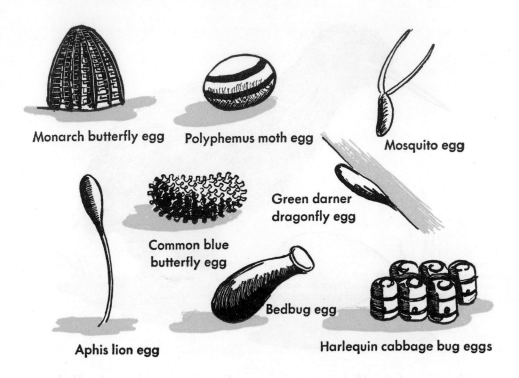

Monarch butterfly egg   Polyphemus moth egg   Mosquito egg

Green darner
dragonfly egg

Common blue
butterfly egg

Bedbug egg

Aphis lion egg   Harlequin cabbage bug eggs

shaped, or cylindrical. The egg of the monarch butterfly looks like a miniature beehive. Some moths have
eggs as flat as a pancake. Bedbug eggs are shaped like
long, narrow sacks. Eggs of the big green darner
dragonfly are like tiny cucumbers. Those of the
walking stick are long and rodlike, just like the adult
insect.

Eggs can be almost any color. Some are transparent. Others are white or black or any other color in
between. They may be lined or splotched, spotted or

peppered with different designs. Special glands in the female animal's egg channel deposit color on the shell of the egg before it is laid.

Color often helps conceal the egg. The color or pattern of bird eggs probably makes them less noticeable when the parent bird is away from the nest. The eggs of the killdeer, which are laid in plain view on the ground, are so splotched and speckled with soft colors that they blend almost perfectly into their background.

The shells of most bird eggs are smooth and hard. Some like the ostrich egg may be pitted. The thickness of the shell can vary from nearly a half inch in the case of the ostrich egg to paper thinness. Bird eggshells are brittle and will break if the egg is dropped.

Most reptile eggs have tough, leathery shells. Fish and amphibian eggs, which are laid in the water, have a soft covering which absorbs water and swells. Insect eggs are usually protected by fairly hard shells, and their surfaces are often elaborately pitted. Some species of insects even lay different kinds of eggs at different times of the year. Eggs laid just before a dry season, for example, may have very thick, hard

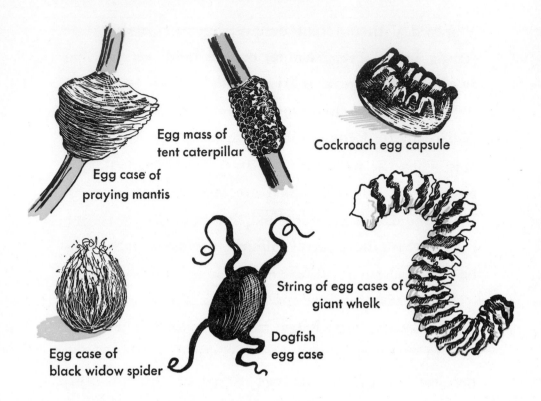

Egg case of praying mantis

Egg mass of tent caterpillar

Cockroach egg capsule

Egg case of black widow spider

Dogfish egg case

String of egg cases of giant whelk

coverings for added protection.

Many animals protect their eggs in cases. Spiders spin a tough silken bag around their eggs while the praying mantis encases its eggs in a frothy liquid which dries into a substance as hard as varnish. The cockroach encloses her eggs in tough envelopes like plastic. Earthworm eggs are in what looks like a capsule. The whelk, a marine mollusc, lays her eggs in a long chain of egg cases.

Why is there so much variety in eggs? The answer lies in the great variety of life itself, and in the many different conditions under which eggs must develop. Each type of egg is well suited to its particular environment.

Care and Incubation of Eggs

Eggs must have favorable conditions for developing and hatching. In a poultry hatchery, incubators keep the eggs at just the right temperature. Wild birds incubate their eggs by sitting on them. The eggs of a mammal are incubated inside the mother's body.

Both mammals and birds maintain a sort of heat-regulating system within their own bodies. Even though the weather is cold, their bodies remain warm. We say they are warm-blooded. To develop properly their eggs have to be kept at this constant body temperature.

All other animals are called cold-blooded. They get their warmth from outside sources: sun-warmed air, for example, or rocks or water. Eggs of cold-blooded animals do not have to be kept warm. Cold-blooded egg-layers usually put their eggs in a suitable place and pay no further attention to them. The time needed for eggs of a particular species to hatch depends on the temperature of their surroundings. Eggs of the spadefoot toad may hatch in as little as five or six days if they are laid in sun-warmed water. If the water is cold, the eggs may take as long as two weeks to hatch.

A few cold-blooded animals stay with their eggs after they have laid them, usually to protect them. Several lizards, the blue-tailed skink among them, curl about their eggs as if brooding them. After basking in the sun, the lizard's body may be warm enough to supply the eggs with some slight additional heat. Several years ago the Reptile Department at the Bronx Zoo received a female python which was coiled tightly around her cluster of eggs. She remained in this position until they hatched. Tests showed that the temperature inside her coils was slightly higher than that of the surrounding air. In this case it can be said that the python was incubating her eggs as well as guarding them.

Most egg-laying reptiles deposit their eggs in the ground or in debris. This hides and protects them.

The female python may coil herself tightly around her eggs.

It also provides fairly steady temperature and moisture. The American alligator goes a step farther than this. She makes a bulky nest of mud and decaying vegetable matter in which she lays her eggs. The temperature inside the nest is warmer than outside, so the eggs are effectively incubated.

Various fish and aquatic vertebrates take care of their eggs in other ways. The males of many fish stay close to their eggs to protect them from hungry robbers. They constantly fan the eggs with their fins, too, and keep a current of fresh water moving around them. The octopus also hovers over her eggs, guarding and aerating them. She regularly cleans and polishes them. This effectively prevents the growth of bacteria which might kill the eggs.

All birds incubate their eggs in one way or another. Many of them, especially among the waterfowl, cover their eggs with feathers and down when they leave the nest. This conceals the eggs and keeps them warm while the parent is away. The female turns the eggs

The octopus guards her eggs, cleaning and polishing them.

frequently. In this way all parts of the egg are exposed evenly to warmth and moisture.

The incubation period varies greatly with different kinds of birds. The eggs of most of our songbirds develop and hatch in twelve to fifteen days. The cowbird's egg hatches after only ten days. Although it is smaller, the egg of the ruby-throated hummingbird takes fourteen days to develop. The eggs of most game birds and waterfowl take three or four weeks to hatch and the king penguin egg takes a little over seven weeks. The patient ostrich may sit on its eggs from forty to sixty days before they hatch. The kiwi has the longest incubation period of all—seventy-five to eighty days. The yolk of a kiwi egg has to be large to nourish the growing embryo for so long.

Most birds do not start to incubate their eggs until they have laid a complete set or clutch. The barn owl, however, starts incubation as soon as the first egg is laid. The female lays an egg every other day and may have as many as six or eight eggs in her clutch. With such an arrangement, the fledgling owl from the first egg may be almost two weeks old when the last one hatches.

A strange family of birds in Australia incubate their

eggs a different way. These are the megapodes, or mound builders. They build huge nests of brush and decayed vegetable matter, like haystacks. The females lay their eggs inside the mound and then let the heat of the sun and the decaying vegetation incubate the eggs for them. As soon as a young mound builder hatches, it makes its way to the surface and goes off alone. It can take care of itself immediately, for it is feathered and can fly almost from the moment it leaves the shell.

Coming Into the World

Birth or hatching is an important event for any baby animal. It marks the end of life within the shell or the mother's body. It means the start of life in the outside world. How is this great change accomplished?

Some larval insects use their jaws to cut openings in the tough shells of their eggs. Then they push their way out or eat the eggshells for their first meal.

Other insect larvae break through the shell with the help of a pointed spine on their back, or a ridge with a sharp edge. Among some insects each egg has a built-in door. This is a weakened section of the shell

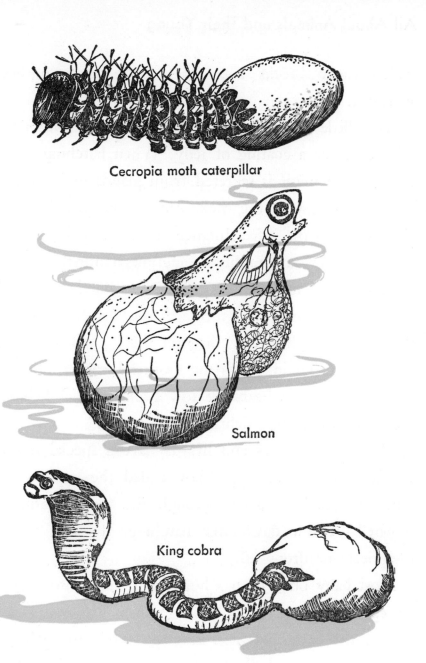

Cecropia moth caterpillar

Salmon

King cobra

Breaking out of the egg is an important event for any animal.

which easily breaks away when the larva pushes against it.

As a little fish or tadpole develops, it squirms and wiggles inside a coating of jelly. When hatching time comes, a chemical is secreted from glands in its head. This helps dissolve the shell. Finally the young tears right through the soft substance surrounding it. Sometimes it comes out headfirst, sometimes tailfirst.

Baby alligators have horny structures on their snouts which help them tear through the eggshell. Then they must dig their way through the packed dirt and vegetable matter in which the mother buried the eggs. When the mother hears the low grunts of her babies, she often clears this debris away herself.

Many baby snakes and lizards have a special tooth at the front of the upper jaw called the egg tooth. They use this to pierce through the tough leathery eggshell. A few days after hatching, the egg tooth disappears or drops off.

Most baby birds have a horny structure, also called an egg tooth, on their beaks. When hatching time comes, the little bird uses the egg tooth to make a tiny break in the shell. Then it begins to peck at the shell with its beak. It doesn't have much room to

Timber rattlesnake

Box tortoise

Bluebird

At birth rattlesnakes are wrapped in a thin membrane. Baby
bluebirds, unlike box tortoises, are helpless when hatched.

maneuver, so it can make only gentle taps. Eventually a small hole is made in the shell, and the first faint peep can be heard.

The hatchling may stop to rest, but soon it is tapping again. At last the egg cracks in two, and the bedraggled little bird tumbles out. Often the parent bird eats the eggshell or carries it away from the nest to dispose of it. No broken shells are left under the nest to attract enemies.

Young of the rattlesnake develop inside the mother's body. When birth time comes, the mother forces the young out, one at a time. Each is wrapped in a soft, thin membrane that is almost transparent. Within a few minutes or hours the young one breaks through the membrane and crawls away. It is fully equipped to face the world on its own.

Baby mammals are also enveloped in birth membranes. When the time of birth comes, muscle contractions dislodge the young from the mother's womb. The baby is then forced down the birth canal and into the outside world, usually headfirst. The enveloping membranes usually break just before the baby emerges or during the birth process.

3. Preparations for the Family

Many fish and aquatic invertebrates simply cast their eggs into the water. Depending on what kind they are, the eggs may float, sink to the bottom or cling to plants. Many are eaten or destroyed. Yet water is the best—the only—place where these eggs could develop. Practically all egg-laying mothers lay their eggs in a place suited to their development. Sometimes they go to great effort to lay their eggs in a particular place.

Snails and garden slugs lay their eggs in dark, moist spots under rocks or debris. There the humidity and temperature are right for their development. Insects usually lay their eggs where the larvae will find a plentiful food supply as soon as they hatch. The big brown monarch butterfly lays her eggs on milkweed, the food plant of her larvae. The black swallowtail lays her eggs on Queen Anne's lace or wild carrot. Grasshoppers and crickets lay their eggs in the ground. There they are protected; and when the young hatch, there is plenty of plant material at hand for their food.

Many female insects have special egg-laying organs called ovipositors on the ends of their abdomens. With these they are able to pierce plant tissues and lay their eggs in special places. Dragonflies lay their eggs in the water. Some parasitic wasps lay their eggs on caterpillars which furnish food for the larvae when they hatch.

Frogs, toads and salamanders often travel long distances overland in order to lay their eggs in the water. The giant marine turtles reverse this journey. They spend their whole lives at sea but come ashore to lay their eggs in a sandy beach. Fresh-water turtles lay their eggs on land too. The turtle mother selects a

The male giant water bug carries his mate's eggs on his back.

spot where she digs a hole. She then lays her eggs in the hole and carefully covers them over with dirt.

Some animals take their eggs along with them wherever they go. Many spiders carry their eggs in silken sacs. The crayfish carries her red eggs on the underside of her abdomen. The male giant water bug carries his mate's eggs on his back. The female marsupial frog of South America also carries her eggs on her back, and in a few species of catfish the female carries her eggs in a fold of skin on her belly or in a fold of her lips.

The Saga of the Salmon and the Eel

Many animals make long trips in order to reach a particular spot or area in which to lay their eggs or bear their young. Every spring our songbirds migrate north from their southern wintering grounds in order to set up housekeeping around us. When we see a redwing teetering on a cattail, we know that a few months ago he was probably swaying on a reed in Argentina, some five or six thousand miles away.

The Alaskan fur seals roam through the broad Pacific every year but return each spring to the Pribilof Islands to bear their young. Many fish also travel long distances in order to lay their eggs in a particular location. Two spectacular examples are the Atlantic salmon and the eel.

Atlantic salmon live the first year or two of their lives in fresh-water streams of Canada, Europe and the British Isles. When they are six to eight inches long, the young salmon start downstream to salt water. For several years they live there, often ranging hundreds of miles through the Atlantic. They grow rapidly on their abundant diet of sea food. After a couple of years of salt-water life, they may be as much as two or three feet long.

Finally the age-old urge to reproduce starts each adult salmon back toward fresh water. By tagging individual salmon, scientists know that a great many of them return to the same streams in which they hatched.

How can a salmon find its way back to its birth-place? One theory is that the fish can recognize the peculiar chemical make-up of familiar water. As the salmon approaches the coastline and swims offshore, it senses minute chemical differences where a river flows into the sea. The fish turns toward the water mixture that is familiar. Up the river it swims, turning into the same tributary and finally into the same stream from which it came originally.

As it swims up river, the salmon struggles through rapids, over falls, past all sorts of dangers. After it leaves the sea, it eats little or nothing. By the time it reaches its destination, it is battered and worn. But at last the journey is finished in some quiet pool. If

A salmon will leap over a waterfall in order to make the journey
back to his birthplace.

the salmon is a female, she starts to build her nest in the riffles by scooping out a shallow trough in the pebbly bottom with her nose and fins. For a week or more she lays her eggs a few hundred at a time in this nest. The male salmon discharges his milt, or sperm cells, over them as soon as they are laid. Then the female stirs up the bottom to cover the eggs. They lie hidden and safe under the pebbles of the stream bed. In the spring the tiny fish hatch out, and the cycle starts all over again.

American and European eels make an even more remarkable trip for the purpose of egg-laying. Their journey is the reverse of the salmon's. Although hatched in the ocean, eels spend most of their adult lives in fresh water. When it is time to mate and lay eggs, the adult eels start their long journey down-stream to the Atlantic Ocean, perhaps passing salmon going the other way.

Once in salt water, the eels swim toward a common breeding ground. Until recently it was not known where this place was. For years scientists dredged with deep-sea nets, trying to trace the eels' journey. They were not able to follow the adults, but netted numbers of young which had hatched in the ocean.

By recovering smaller and smaller eels farther and farther out at sea, they finally found the breeding area. It was the Sargasso Sea between Bermuda and the West Indies. Both American and European eels come here to lay their eggs at great depths and then to die.

The larval eel is a tiny flat creature.

Eel eggs hatch into tiny flat creatures quite unlike adult eels. As the larvae grow, they gradually rise to the surface and start their long journey back to fresh water. American eels take less than two years for the journey back to America's rivers. European eels take three years for their trip. Hatched in the same ocean area, how do the tiny European eels know how to get back to Europe, and the American eels back to American streams? No one knows for sure.

This Spot Is Mine!

When a male bird sings in the spring, he is telling the world that this spot is his. He is especially warning other males of the same species to keep away from his territory. And finally, he is advertising his presence to prospective mates. When he has courted and won a female, she builds a nest in his territory, and they raise a family there.

The males of many migratory birds generally arrive at the breeding grounds several weeks before the females. Each male picks out a territory and establishes its boundaries by singing and chasing intruders. If he is successful in defending the area against all comers, that is his territory. In the case of songbirds, this territory may be as much as one or two acres, or as little as a back yard. With birds that nest in colonies, such as gulls or gannets, the territory may be only a few square feet. The territories of birds of prey, such as the great horned owl or bald eagle, may cover several square miles. The territories of different

By his singing, the male redwing warns off rivals.

species may overlap, or one may be within the other. There is no conflict if the species are not rivals for food.

Mammals stake out living and breeding territories for themselves in much the same way that birds do. The territory of a mouse may be a very small patch of ground while the territory of a big meat-eating animal like a mountain lion or a tiger may cover many square miles. Male Alaskan fur seals may roam all over the ocean the rest of the year, but they have very sharply limited territories during the breeding season.

Every spring the fur seals migrate to the Pribilof Islands to raise their families. The breeding males always arrive before the females. With many disputes and fights each bull establishes a beachhead for himself. As long as he stays on his own territory and defends it, he is the king of the realm. If he trespasses on a neighbor's land, however, he is challenged immediately. Boundaries change back and forth, but finally the conquests are well established.

When the females arrive, another contest starts as each male tries to induce as many females as he can to come up on his beach and join his harem. After more fighting and wife-stealing, an uneasy peace is established. The females give birth to their young almost immediately. These are raised in the territory of the male who won their mother. Frequently the mothers go out to swim and hunt for fish, but the males stay on their beachheads to guard their territory and young. For several months the male does not eat at all. By the fall the young are weaned and have learned how to swim. Then the whole great herd leaves to take up their wandering life at sea for

The bull fur seal guards his harem of females and their young.

another year. In the meantime, the male has mated with each female in his harem. They will bear his pups next year.

There's No Place Like Home

Some animals have no fixed home at all and lead a wandering existence. But for a great many animals, home is the center of family life, just as it is with people. It is the place where the young are born and reared, until they are mature enough to leave. Home for a newly hatched sea bird or a baby fur seal may be only a tiny section of rocky beach. For a cotton-tail rabbit it may be a shallow indentation in the ground. To a pigeon it may be a crude nest of twigs. But no matter how crude or simply constructed, it is home base to that baby animal.

Many insects, such as ants and bees, make elaborate underground homes, with countless corridors, tunnels, food chambers, nest chambers and nurseries. African termites build skyscrapers as much as ten or more feet high, in which they live and carry on their activities. Mud dauber wasps construct mud or adobe houses in which to raise their young. Other wasps make paper houses of bark or other plant fibers which they chew up and press into thin sheets. The big round nests of hornets are of this type.

Some larval insects make their own protective shelters. Colonies of tent caterpillars spin tentlike, silken webs on wild cherry and domestic fruit trees. This serves as a protective home base for the caterpillars. Bagworms, the caterpillars of another kind of moth, construct durable individual bags for themselves, made of silk covered with evergreen needles. Everywhere they go they carry these protective shelters with them. If a bird tries to eat one, the bagworm simply retreats into his house.

The aquatic larvae of caddis flies—which are close relatives of moths and butterflies—construct similar shelters. One species makes a long cylindrical house of sand and pebbles. Another uses tiny snail shells exclusively. Still others use pieces of leaves or pine needles, which they fasten together with silk. Various fish make shelters for their eggs, and so do a few amphibians and reptiles.

We could hardly call all of these structures homes. But with birds and mammals the construction of homes is the rule rather than the exception.

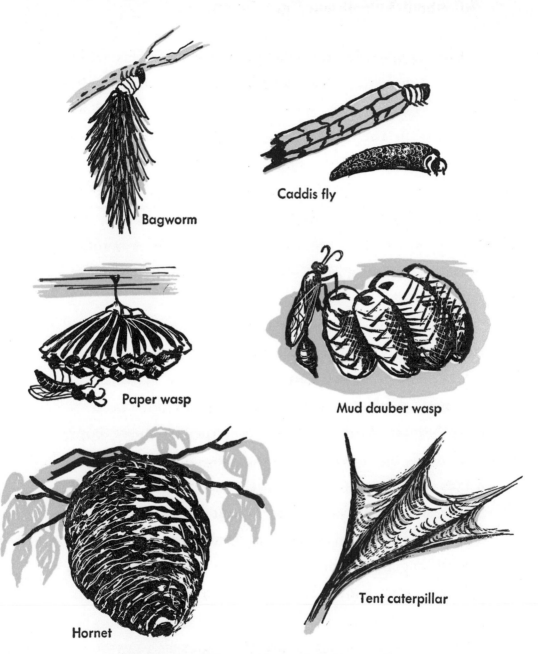

Bagworm

Caddis fly

Paper wasp

Mud dauber wasp

Hornet

Tent caterpillar

Insects make different kinds of shelters or houses.

Birds are by far the champion nest builders of the animal kingdom. Some sea and shore birds, to be sure, simply lay their eggs on the ground or in simple depressions in the sand. But most birds build nests of one sort or another, some of them very elaborate. Bird nests come in all sizes and shapes and are constructed from many different kinds of materials. By observing the shape of a nest, the materials it is made of and its location, you can usually identify the bird that built it.

The catbird, for example, builds a nest of coarse twigs, usually in dense foliage close to the ground. The Baltimore oriole constructs a lightly woven sac-like nest of plant fibers suspended from the tips of a high branch. Most warblers construct compact cup-like nests in notches of branches. The bald eagle makes a huge platform of sticks, sometimes as much as ten or twelve feet deep and eight or ten feet across. The tailor bird makes its nest between leaves, neatly stitched together with plant fibers. Some sunbirds build covered nests with little porticos or sheltering roofs over the entrance.

Twigs, grass and leaves are the materials most commonly used for the outer walls of birds' nests. Clay

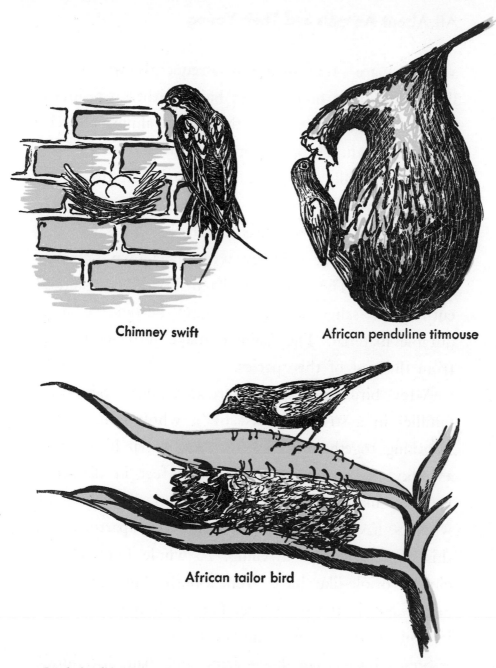

Chimney swift

African penduline titmouse

African tailor bird

Birds build nests of many sizes and shapes. The African pendu-line titmouse has a bag-shaped nest with a tunnel-like opening.

and mud are often used too. Frequently the nest is lined with plant down, horse hair, feathers or similar material. Goldfinches make their nests almost entirely of thistledown. Hummingbirds use plant down of all kinds and usually cover the outside of their tiny nests with lichens held together by spider silk. Chimney swifts fashion nests of sticks which they plaster to the sides of a wall or chimney with their own saliva as the adhesive. The oriental swift makes its nest almost entirely of saliva which dries and becomes a hard durable material. The Chinese make bird's-nest soup from the nest of this species.

A few birds, such as the African weavers, raise their families in a structure used by a whole community. Working together, a flock of these social birds build a bulky nest which may be many feet in diameter. It looks like a haystack in a treetop. Each pair of weavers has an individual burrow-like apartment in this huge collective dwelling. A whole flock of caciques, oriole-like birds from South America, often build nests in the same tree. Each pair builds its own individual hanging nest, however.

Some birds, like kingfishers and bank swallows, make their homes in burrows in the ground. Others, such as the woodpeckers, drill holes in trees in which to make their nests. They use their strong beaks to hammer or drill out the cavity. You can often tell what kind of woodpecker made the hole just by the size and shape of its entrance. A number of other kinds of birds, including the parrots, nest in holes in trees too, but usually they just take over a hollow that has already been made by some other animal.

Makers of Burrows and Lodges

A few mammals make pretty good nests too. Gray squirrels often raise their young in bulky leaf nests which they build in a treetop.

Wood mice sometimes take over an old bird nest as their home, or they may make their own nest of grass, plant down or other soft material. These nests may be located in trees or bushes, in the ground, in hollow logs, or even in some old shoe in a closed-up summer cottage. Wood rats of the Western states sometimes build bulky nests in the trees. A number of families may live in one nest, which has many entrances and compartments. Some rooms are used for sleeping, some for storing food, others for nurseries.

Still others are places for depositing waste materials.

But it is in building burrows that mammals really shine. Practically all kinds of rodents—rats, mice, ground squirrels, gophers and the like—make burrows. So do such different kinds of mammals as skunks and weasels, shrews and moles, pangolins and aardvarks. The burrow may be nothing more than a short tunnel with a nest chamber at its end. Or it may be quite elaborate, like that of the woodchuck, which is an excellent burrower. Its home is usually excavated on a hillside. It always has two and sometimes three entrances. The main tunnel may slope downward for many feet and have several branching corridors that end in rooms. The young are raised in a soft nest of plant material in one of these chambers.

Probably the most remarkable burrow is that built by a prairie dog. The entrance is surrounded on all sides by a built-up cone of earth which protects it from the flash floods of the prairies. The entrance tunnel goes almost straight down for eight to fourteen feet or more before it turns parallel to the surface. Several tunnels with nest chambers at their ends branch off from this main corridor.

Prairie dogs are sociable little beasts. In the past,

Prairie dogs build remarkably deep burrows which often have
many nest chambers or pockets.

The busy beaver builds elaborate lodges and dams.

hundreds of thousands have lived together in great prairie-dog cities. At present very few prairie-dog towns are left, for these little rodents have been largely exterminated over much of their former range.

Among the most elaborate of all mammal homes are the lodges which beavers build. These are always located in the water, either in a natural pond or in

These he makes from trees and branches he cuts down.

one which the beavers have made. The lodge is usually a bulky affair, ten or fifteen feet across and five or six feet above the water. It is built of logs and branches from trees which the beavers fell with their sharp teeth. Each piece is dragged or floated into place. Mud is used to plaster the openings between the logs. All entrances are under water.

Inside, the floor of the lodge is built up a few inches above water level. Here the beaver family lives snug and protected all winter through. There is usually an opening or chimney left in the roof for ventilation. Though ice on the pond may be many inches thick, the beavers have plenty of stored food in the form of green branches which they anchored in the stream bed the summer and fall before.

As many as a dozen beavers may live in one lodge. Usually there is an old male with several females and their young of a year or two before. When spring comes and new babies are due, the young from the previous litter leave the lodge to set up housekeeping for themselves. The new babies are born in a soft nest of bark and shavings on one side of the floor of the lodge.

4. Providing Food for Hungry Mouths

Very few insects take care of their own young. Usually they just lay their eggs and then go on their way. However, they are careful to place the eggs where the larvae are most likely to find a good food supply. A few of them even provide food for their young.

The cicada killer, one of the solitary wasps, is one of these. This striking-looking big insect excavates separate burrows or nest chambers in the ground for each of its eggs. After it has finished a burrow, it hunts a cicada with which to stock the larder. When it finds one, it stings it, paralyzing but not killing it. The cicada killer then straddles its victim and carries it back to her nest chamber. She then lays a single egg on the paralyzed cicada and seals the chamber. When the larval cicada killer hatches, it has a huge supply of fresh cicada meat to eat as it develops.

The long-tailed ichneumon fly reverses this procedure. Instead of bringing food to the spot where she lays her eggs, she places her eggs where the food is. When she is ready to lay her eggs, she searches over the trunk and branches of a likely looking tree until she detects the burrows of the larvae of the pigeon horntail beetle. These are an inch or two beneath the surface of the wood. Perhaps she hears the grubs moving about. Perhaps her tapping antennae detect the hollow burrow.

Raising her abdomen at an angle, she places the tip of her threadlike ovipositor at right angles to the wood and starts to drill. Slowly it works its way through as much as two inches of wood. When it reaches the burrow of the grub, the egg is laid in that burrow. When the ichneumon larva hatches, it

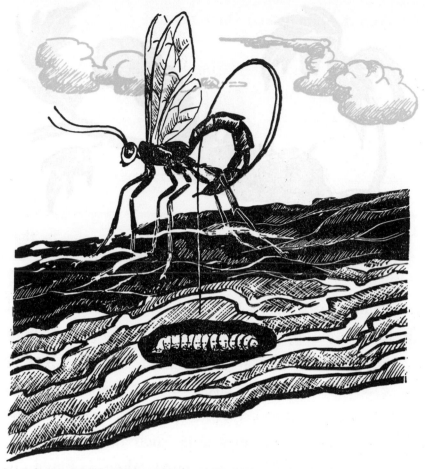

An ichneumon fly bores into wood to lay eggs in the burrow of a pigeon horntail larva.

can eat the larva of the other insect.

Certain other species of ichneumons lay their eggs directly on moth or butterfly caterpillars. When the larvae hatch, they promptly burrow into the caterpillar and start to feed on its insides. If you have ever seen a big horned tomato worm with a number of

Tiny white ovals on the back of a tomato worm may be the
cocoons of ichneumon larvae.

tiny white ovals on its back, you've seen the work of
an ichneumon fly. The white ovals are the cocoons
of the ichneumon larvae. They feast on the insides of
the caterpillar until they are fully developed and then
burrow back to the surface to spin their cocoons. The
caterpillar, of course, dies after such treatment.

Wasps, bees and ants are outstanding examples of
insects that take care of their young until they become adults. Honeybees are among the most interesting of all. As you know, bees live together in
swarms or hives. The queen bee lays an egg in one
of the six-sided wax cells of the honeycomb. When
the egg hatches, it is fed by nursemaid worker bees,
who give it bee bread—a partially digested mixture of
honey and pollen. The nurses eat this food, partially

digest it, and then disgorge it for the young. When the white legless grub reaches its full growth, it pupates. After a few days it emerges from the pupa— a new worker ready to take its place in the life of the hive.

Worker bees are stunted females. They cannot lay eggs or reproduce. Practically all bees in a hive are workers. They perform many duties, and each worker does most or all of them in a set order. For the first few days after she has hatched, a worker is a nurse-maid, feeding and caring for the white grubs in their individual cells. After a few days of this kitchen detail, she graduates to making wax for new cells while younger workers do the nursemaid job. After a tour of duty as a wax-maker, the worker becomes a "fanner" stationed near the entrance to ventilate the hive by buzzing her wings. After this, the worker becomes a field bee. Every day she goes out to collect pollen and nectar—food for the whole colony. For the rest of her life she performs this work.

Once in a while, when the colony gets very big, the workers may build a number of very large cells. The larvae which hatch from eggs in these cells are fed a special food called "royal jelly," and they develop into other queen bees. Just before the new queens are ready to hatch, the old queen, surrounded by a portion of her swarm, flies away to start a new colony. The first new queen to hatch is allowed to open all the other royal cells and sting the unhatched queens to death. There can be only one queen! After a short mating flight, the new queen comes back to start her egg-laying duties, just as the queen before her did.

Birds Are Busy From Dawn to Dusk

If you have watched a pair of songbirds raising a family, you know how busy the parent birds are. From sunup to sundown they are collecting food for their hungry nestlings. Sometimes the growing youngsters eat more than their own weight of food daily.

A vireo has been observed making forty-five trips to its nest with food in a single hour. But that is nothing in comparison to a house wren that was counted making fifteen hundred trips in fifteen hours.

Within their nests, baby birds are far from peaceful. The strongest fledglings usually push the weaker ones aside in their eagerness for food, and the parent obligingly fills the nearest mouth. If the nest is jarred

The mother chickadee continues to feed her young.

or brushed against, the nestling songbird raises its head instinctively and opens its beak. When the parent bird lights on the edge of the nest, the bobbing heads come up as though by signal, and gaping beaks open wide. The throats of baby birds are usually bright yellow or red, bordered with a whitish line along the edge of the beak—easy targets for their parent's aim.

This wide-open mouth is a triggering sight to the adult bird too. Instinctively the parent stuffs food down the nearest, most demanding gullet. If the young bird is so stuffed that it cannot swallow, the parent obligingly takes the food out and tries another beak. Nothing must be wasted. The stronger nestlings get served first, and the weaker ones have to wait until the bigger brothers and sisters are filled.

From the day they hatch, young game birds and waterfowl are able to follow their mother and pick up their own food. The mother bird finds food for them and calls them to come and get especially tempting morsels. Listen to a hen with chicks. She has many different calls, almost a language with which she talks to her brood. Calm clucking seems to help keep the brood together. Danger calls cause the young to run under her wings for protection. If the mother calls to "come and get it," the youngsters flock eagerly to the spot where she is scratching.

Among the birds of prey, the father bird often does most of the hunting and bringing home of food— usually a freshly slain small mammal, bird or fish. He hands the food over to his mate, and she tears it apart, taking what she wants for herself and giving the rest to the youngsters. When her babies are very young, she may tear the meat into small morsels which they can swallow whole. As they grow, however, they learn to tear the food apart themselves and engage in many fierce tugs of war.

Some birds feed their young by disgorging partially digested food for the babies to eat. Hummingbirds thrust their long beaks down the throats of their young to pump liquid food into them. A pelican baby reverses this procedure. It looks as though it is trying to crawl down its parent's throat as it struggles to get the partially digested fish which the adult coughs up.

The baby pelican takes its food out of the parent's pouch.

77

The king penguin partially digests food for its woolly youngster.

King penguins feed their single offspring in a some-what similar manner. When the young bird utters its food call, the parent bird, with much twisting of its neck and gulping, coughs up some partially digested fish. The woolly youngster then picks the morsels up from the side of the parent's beak. Pigeons feed their young on "pigeon milk," a predigested food which looks like thick milk and is formed in the adult bird's crop.

Among those grotesque and enormous-billed birds, the hornbills of Africa and Asia, the male has a strange part to play in raising the young. His mate seals her-self up in her nest in a hollow tree with a mixture of mud and dung which hardens like plaster. She leaves an entrance hole just big enough for the tip of her huge beak. While the imprisoned female incu-bates her eggs and the young are growing up, the male faithfully brings food to her and the young.

Some male hornbills regurgitate their food offerings in neat packages, enclosed in thin sacs. The sac is the inner lining of the male's crop, the place where the food was stored after the male swallowed it. This lining of the crop is easily shed, a special adaptation which enables the hornbill to give his mate a good supply of food at one time. A new lining is formed almost immediately to take the place of the one that was shed.

While her young are growing up, the female moults and grows new feathers. At last the family is ready to leave the nest. When the wall sealing the nest opening is broken down, the female and young come out as fat as butter balls. But by this time the poor male is usually quite thin and ragged after his hard work collecting food for his family.

Milk, the Perfect Food

The only animals which are able to produce milk and to nurse their young are the mammals. Milk is stored in the female mammal's milk glands and secreted through her teats or nipples.

Mammals can be divided into three main groups, depending on how and where their young develop. The most primitive group are those which lay eggs, like the platypus. Then there are the marsupials or pouched animals, like the kangaroo and opossum. Their young are born in a very immature state and develop further in their mother's pouch. All others

The male hornbill supplies his imprisoned mate with food.

are placental mammals, which develop inside the mother's body, connected with it by a placenta. All three kinds of mammals produce milk and nurse their young.

After a baby mammal is weaned, its mother's milk supply dries up. She does not produce milk again until the birth of her next young one. As the birth time approaches, a new supply of milk begins. It is formed from fats, sugars, proteins and minerals plus water from the mother's blood stream. The first milk that the mother produces is especially rich in proteins and is called colostrum. The newborn baby mammal gets this special milk when it is weakest and most vulnerable. After a day or two the colostrum is replaced by the mother's regular milk. Cow's milk is quite similar to human milk. That is why human babies can be given cow's milk if their own mother is unable to nurse them.

The arrangements of the mother's milk glands on her body and the way the babies nurse vary greatly with different species. Mother monkeys have two milk glands situated on their breasts, between their two arms. Usually the mother holds the baby monkey or it clings to her while it nurses. Elephants also have

two nipples between their front legs. The baby
elephant is just tall enough to stand between its
mother's legs and reach her teats. It does not suck

The baby elephant takes milk through its mouth, not its trunk.

milk through its trunk as some people think. It curls the trunk aside or over its forehead and suckles with its mouth the way any other baby mammal does.

Hoofed animals such as cattle, deer and antelope usually stand while their young nurse. Their milk is stored in a bag or udder between the female's hind legs. This bag may have one or more compartments in it, each equipped with a nipple. A cow usually has a four-part milk bag.

The whale's two milk glands are located toward the rear of her body. When her young wants to nurse, she rolls on her side and squeezes powerful muscles which force the thick milk out. The baby whale nuzzles close to her nipple and gulps down the nourishing liquid.

The milk of some mammals contains the various food elements in quite different proportions from cow's milk. Whales and seals, for example, have milk that is very rich in fats. Some seal milk has ten times as much fat as cow's milk. In their cold-water environment, baby seals and whales need more fat than most mammal babies to provide fuel for insulation and body heat.

How long the young will nurse depends on many

Like most hoofed animals, the bison calf stands while it nurses.

things—how fast the baby develops, how soon it
learns to eat other food, how long the mother continues to supply milk, and how soon she has young
again. The longer it takes the youngster to mature,
the longer the nursing period. Sooner or later, however, the young mammal has to be weaned onto
other food.

With foxes, wolves, coyotes and other wild dogs,
the weaning process is a gradual one. While the
young are nursing, the father often acts as chief

huntsman and brings meat home for his mate. When the young are old enough to walk about and take notice, the mother introduces them to solid food. At first she regurgitates some partially digested meat for the youngsters to sample. She often gives them a bone or piece of meat to smell and play with. This is great sport for the youngsters, who stalk the bone and pounce on it. They tear at it with their tiny needle-sharp teeth and growl furiously while the mother watches proudly. Her young are getting the taste of their natural food. Soon they are eating shreds of flesh which they tear from the bone. When they are ready, the mother takes the young out on short hunting expeditions with her. By watching her, they learn how to locate prey and stalk it. Finally the great day comes when one of her pups pounces on his first field mouse or other small rodent. He has learned how to hunt for himself.

5. Family Life and Care

Male birds often help with raising the family. But with mammals it is usually the mother that brings up the babies while papa goes his merry, carefree way. Most fish do not give much care to their young. But when they do, it is the male who usually builds the nest and plays nursemaid to the young.

The brightly colored little sunfish is a very good father. With his fins and mouth, he prepares a shallow bowl-shaped nest in a sandy bottom. He then induces as many females as he can to come and lay their eggs in his nursery. Once the female has laid her eggs, her part in child-raising is finished. The male's work has just started. He protects the eggs, guarding them against any fish or other animal that might try to harm them. When the young hatch out, he stays on guard near by until they can swim by themselves.

One time while standing in shallow water near the shore of a lake, I felt something hit my toe. A male sunfish was charging at my foot. Repeatedly he rushed in and tried to drive me away. Searching the sandy bottom, I spied his nest near by. I had come too close to suit him, and he was telling me: "No trespassing!"

The stickleback is another model father. He skillfully builds a nest of algae and other water plants which he sticks together with a secretion from his kidneys. Then he goes courting and leads or herds a female over toward the nest. Once there he practically shoves her into it. As soon as she has laid her eggs, he fertilizes them and then goes out to find another female. When the nest is full of eggs, he stands by, guarding them and fanning them with his fins to aerate them. When the young hatch, he stays near by until they can look after themselves.

**After the female stickleback lays her eggs in a nest of algae
and other water plants, the father guards them.**

Another protective father is the Siamese fighting
fish—a colorful tropical beauty. The male of this
species builds a nest for his mate's eggs by blowing
bubbles which float up to the surface in a large frothy
mass. When this bubble nest is ready, the male flashes
his brilliant gill coverings at the female, raises his
showy fins and does everything in his power to put
her in the right egg-laying mood. At last the female
is stimulated to lay her eggs. As soon as each egg is
laid and fertilized, the male carries it in his mouth to

the protective bubble nest. If an egg should fall out and sink, he is right there to swoop down and retrieve it.

A very high type of paternal care is shown by some of the fresh-water fish called cichlids. One famous student of animal behavior tells of a male

A male sea horse expels his young from his brood pouch.

cichlid which acted for all the world like a fussy old nursemaid. This father fish herded his young together in a school and kept them from straying. In the evening he guided them back to the nest with painstaking care. If any tried to dash off, as children often do when faced with bedtime, he picked them up in his mouth and swam back to the nest to deposit them.

Some male fish protect their eggs by carrying them about with them until they hatch. The male sea horse has a brood pouch on the front part of his abdomen in which to carry his eggs. The eggs, 150 to 200 of them, become imbedded in the thick walls lining the pouch. There they develop for about forty-five days before hatching. When the young sea horses have hatched, the father expels the young from their nursery, often with considerable difficulty.

Some frogs and toads have wonderful ways of caring for their young. The males of certain species actually carry the eggs laid by the female. For example, the male midwife toad carries his mate's fertilized eggs entangled in his hind feet. The male Darwin frog of South America carries the eggs in his enlarged vocal sacs until the tadpoles have emerged and developed into small frogs. The father Surinam toad does not

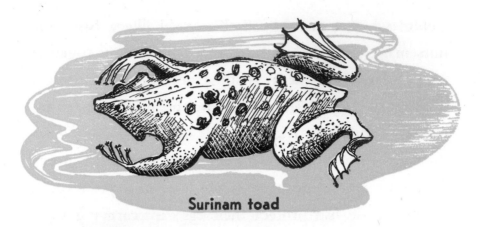

Surinam toad

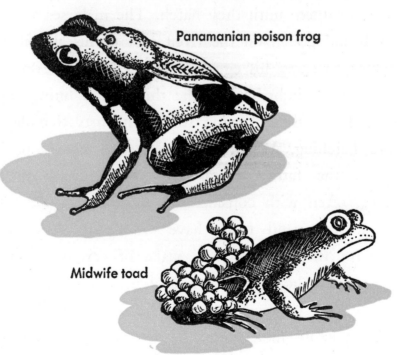

Panamanian poison frog

Midwife toad

The female Surinam toad (top) carries her eggs in her back. The tadpole of the Panamanian poison frog (center) sometimes travels on the father's back. The male midwife toad (bottom) carries his mate's eggs entangled in his hind feet.

carry the eggs himself, but he presses them into little pits or pouches on his mate's back. The eggs sink in and are held in place by a sticky secretion. A lid forms over each egg. The young hatch from the eggs and develop into tiny toads before pushing their way out.

Another curious species is the Panamanian poison frog. This is a small, brilliantly colored species only an inch long. The eggs are laid in temporary pools in ditches or even in the rain water which gathers in a cup-shaped leaf. After the young hatch, and before the temporary pool dries up, the male frog carries the tadpoles to more permanent pools, usually in hollow tree trunks. On the journey each polliwog hangs onto his back with its mouth.

Bird Families

Birds show all sorts of degrees and kinds of family life. With pheasants and other game birds, one male will mate with as many females as he can attract. This accomplished, he leaves the nest-building, incubating and all other duties of parenthood to the females. With prairie chickens, one hen mates with a number of males, but here again, she gets saddled with the work of raising the family.

Anis, birds found in Central and South America, might be called communistic in their nesting habits. Together, a flock of anis build a large, crude, platform-like nest in a tree. All the females lay their eggs there, and various members of the flock incubate them in what seems a haphazard arrangement. When the young hatch, all the members of the group take part in feeding them.

Most birds have only one mate at a time. The Canada goose, the mute swan, the bald eagle and others mate for life. Often the same pair of birds will come back to the same nest or nesting area year after year. Most songbirds have only one mate at a time, but sometimes they have a different mate each nesting season.

When birds live in pairs, the parents generally work as a team in incubating the eggs and taking care of the young. They may work alternate shifts or each may specialize. Among the flightless birds—ostriches, rheas, emus and cassowaries—the male bird does most of the work. He usually incubates the eggs and feeds and protects the young. Among hawks, the female does most of the incubating, while the male bird does most of the hunting for both of them. With the

The male ostrich does most of the taking care of his young.

nightjar, the female is in such haste to have another brood that she often lays a second clutch of eggs and starts to incubate them while her first brood still needs care. Then the father nightjar takes over the care of the older chicks.

Many sea birds, such as gannets and gulls, regularly nest in vast colonies. Often there are hundreds of nests in a space the size of the average front yard. The birds have to get along with each other, and generally they do it about as well as a group of people. There are lots of minor quarrels, but generally nothing too serious.

Chimney swifts nest in colonies, too, building individual nests in chimneys or belfries. Purple martins like the sociability of many families together in martin houses of many apartments. But with all of these colonies, each pair takes care of its own young.

A few birds avoid the trouble of incubating eggs and raising their own young. They let other birds do the job for them. The European cuckoo is famous for this. The female cuckoo first locates a suitable nest of some unsuspecting victim. Then she waits until the rightful occupants of the nest are both absent. Quick as a wink she slips in and lays an egg in as little time as eight seconds. When she leaves, she usually carries in her beak one of the eggs she found in the nest.

The victims of this egg-swapping trick may notice the strange egg in their nest and suspect that something is wrong. But they usually incubate the cuckoo egg along with their own. Chances are that the young cuckoo egg will hatch out before the other eggs do. Then, as if to insure that it gets the best of everything, the young cuckoo often hoists the other unhatched eggs over the side of the nest. If its foster brothers hatch, it may do the same thing to them, for it is bigger and stronger than they are. The foster parents feed and raise the intruder as faithfully as though it were their own.

Our native cowbirds frequently invade the nests of birds smaller than themselves, such as sparrows, warblers and vireos. Sometimes a cowbird egg may be left in the nest of a robin or other larger songbird. The incubation period for cowbird eggs is only ten days, so the young cowbird usually hatches out before the natural offspring.

Not all birds stand for this invasion of their homes. Robins sometimes pierce cowbird eggs that they find in their nest and throw them out. Wrens often do the same. When the yellow warbler finds a cowbird egg in its nest, it customarily builds a new nest layer on top of the old one, sealing over the cowbird egg as well as its own eggs.

How Birds Protect Their Young

Birds will go to great extremes to protect their young. To defend their babies, they will attack an intruder they would not dream of approaching other-

When a hawk swoops down, the ruffed grouse gives an alarm.

wise. A mother hen, alert and defiant, stands up to a cat or dog in defense of her chicks. If we get too close to a robin's nest and young, the parents flutter frantically about, uttering loud piercing cries of alarm. Sometimes they fly so close that their wings brush against us. Anyone who has ever approached a swan's nest knows how threatening these birds can be. Arching their necks and hissing fiercely, the parent birds advance to attack. They strike out viciously with their

In the water, young grebes often ride on their mother's back.

beaks and wings, ready to defend their eggs or young with their lives.

Some birds do their best to hide their young or draw attention away from them when danger approaches. When a mother quail gives the "scatter and be still" signal, all her tiny chicks seem to vanish. As they crouch among the jungle of field vegetation, motionless as statues, their fuzzy, spotted little bodies blend perfectly with the background. If they know their lesson, they do not move until the danger has passed. If danger threatens a mother grebe in the water with her young, she will dive with them tucked under her wings.

Some birds resort to tricks to deceive their enemies. A female killdeer will sit motionless on her eggs until an enemy is almost on top of her. Then off she flops, moving uncertainly just ahead of the threat. She does her best to divert attention from her eggs and to her-

The killdeer will often pretend to be injured in order to divert attention from her eggs.

self. She will drag her wing and give every indication of being severely wounded. She keeps just ahead of the enemy, being careful always to stay out of reach. When the threat has been lured far enough away, she abandons her tricks and flies off. Sometimes a male ostrich does the same sort of thing to draw enemies away from his young or eggs. If this fails, he may turn on the enemy and make it run away from him. An aroused ostrich can be a fierce opponent.

The most critical time for young birds, especially songbirds, is the period just after they leave the nest. They are too big and active to stay in the nest, but too inexperienced to take care of themselves. They have not yet learned how to fly very well and are easy prey for all sorts of animals. They still do not know much about how to find their own food. The anxious parent birds are here, there and everywhere— looking after their scattered offspring. They flutter over one timid youngster as it tries its own wings. They feed another one in a nearby bush. They call to a daring one which has flown some distance away. They are everywhere at once as the young learn how to meet the everyday problems of bird life. Within a day or so the young are feeding themselves and flying easily and strongly. Then at last they take off on their own.

The Platypus, Strangest Mammal of All

The only egg-layers among the mammals are the duck-billed platypus and the spiny anteaters, or echidnas. They are the most primitive of all mammals and are very strange creatures in their appearance and in the way they bear their young.

The platypus is found only in parts of Eastern Australia and Tasmania. It has a flat leathery beak shaped much like that of a duck. There is no question of its being a mammal, however, for it is covered with soft dense fur and produces milk with which it nurses its young.

Platypuses live in burrows in the banks of streams. They usually sleep during the day. At night they gather worms, crustaceans and other small animals from the stream bottoms with their flat beaks. The platypus does its courting in the water too. When the time comes, the female prepares a burrow, in which she excavates a nest chamber. She makes a soft bed of leaves and grass in this. When all is ready, she retires into it, plugging the entrances with mud. Here she lays her eggs. Usually there are two, but sometimes only one. The eggs are about three-quarters of an inch in diameter, round, and a dirty parchment color. They have sticky leathery shells which dent easily like reptile eggs. The mother platypus curls around the eggs, brooding them. She does not leave the nest until the eggs are hatched about six days later.

Baby platypuses are tiny creatures—blind, helpless and almost hairless. The milk of the mother platypus oozes from pores on her abdomen, a drop or two at a time, and the young immediately begin to nurse. The babies develop quite slowly. It is a month before they open their eyes. By this time they are covered with a very fine soft coat of fur.

The female platypus is a devoted mother and stays with her young for many weeks. She leaves them only to hunt for food for herself. The young are nearly six months old and practically as big as she is before they venture out of the nest.

Two Australian naturalists studied platypuses for many years. One of them kept a pair of tame duckbills and observed their remarkable courtship and nest-building. By digging down and putting an external window on the brood chamber, he could open the burrow and study developments within. A baby platypus was raised successfully.

In April, 1947, the same naturalist brought three platypuses to the Bronx Zoo in New York where I was on the staff. Although one died after several years, the other two—Cecil and Penelope—flourished

The platypus does its courting in water.

there for ten years. In the summer of 1953 they engaged in courtship activities, and there was great excitement at the zoo and in the newspapers. Penelope was soon acting as though she was an expectant mother. She dug furiously in her earth bank, and we hoped she was building a nest chamber. She ate ravenously, as expectant mothers do. Each day she polished off her daily rations of earthworms, crayfish and coddled eggs and looked around for more. She carried piles of eucalyptus leaves into her burrow—to make a nest, we hoped. Finally she placed a plug of clay at the entrance of her burrow and disappeared.

Day after day went by with no sign of Penelope. We thought she was curled up with her eggs, incubating them far underground. Six days after she had disappeared, she appeared again, and lit into her increased rations with an enormous appetite. We were sure that she had one or more babies in her underground nest chamber. All that summer we looked forward to the great day when she would appear with them in tow. October came and went, but no baby platypuses appeared. November arrived with frosty nights. We would have to take the platypuses in for the winter before it got too cold.

Finally, we dug into the clay bank to probe its secrets. Newspaper reporters and photographers stood by, waiting for the news. After two hours of hard digging, Penelope was uncovered in her underground burrow—but no babies! In desperate search, every bit of earth was removed from the clay bank. There was nothing more. Penelope had fooled us all summer long.

Echidnas, the other egg-laying mammals, are covered with strong sharp spines and have long tubular snouts. The female broods her eggs in a maternal pouch which develops on her underside during the

The echidna or spiny anteater is covered with sharp spines.

breeding season. She carries the young in this pouch also until they begin to develop spines. Then she leaves them in a nest in a hollow log while she goes out to forage.

Mammals With Built-in Baby Seats

Probably the best-known marsupial is the kangaroo. At one time or another practically everyone has seen a kangaroo at the zoo with a bright-eyed baby peering out of her pouch. It is riding in style in its custom-built cradle like a papoose snugly encased in its wrappings.

Most marsupials, like the kangaroo, are native to Australia. There are a great many different kinds. There are marsupial moles, marsupial mice, marsupial dogs, marsupial cats and many others. They are not really moles or mice or dogs or cats like those we know, but they look like them and have the same general habits and food preferences. All have pouches in which their young are sheltered.

Marsupial babies have an extremely short period of development within their mother's body. The new-born young are tiny undeveloped creatures. Just as

Baby Virginia opossums nurse in their mother's pouch.

premature human babies are sheltered in incubators, the tiny undeveloped marsupial babies are sheltered after birth in their mother's own incubator, her pouch. Sometimes there are many babies in one litter, as is the case with the Virginia opossum. Kangaroos, however, usually have only one young at a time.

A full-grown great red kangaroo is a big powerful animal which may stand five feet high. Yet at birth its baby is less than an inch long—about the size of a newborn mouse. Its eyes are not open, its ears have not developed, and its hind limbs are still little more than tiny stubs. Only the forelimbs are developed enough for the baby to use in crawling. As soon as it is born, the baby crawls up its mother's abdomen toward her pouch. The mother usually licks a moist path through the fur on her abdomen, to ease the youngster's journey. She is in a sitting position, with her tail tucked under and in front of her. Instinctively the baby goes in the right direction. It moves along hand over hand through the forest of fur. In a few minutes it reaches its destination and crawls into the pouch.

Some observers insist they have seen a mother kangaroo pick up her newborn young in her mouth and insert it into the pouch. This may happen occasionally, but it is not the usual method.

Once inside the pouch, the baby searches for a nipple. As soon as he finds one, he fastens on to it. The nipple swells up inside the baby's mouth, and for some weeks the little marsupial is more or less firmly attached. The baby develops inside the pouch, as completely sheltered and protected as it was before it was born. The mother kangaroo keeps her pouch neat and clean by licking it out daily.

After several months the young kangaroo has developed enough to be detached from the nipple. Its eyes are now open, and it is covered with soft fur. It often pokes its head out of the pouch to see what is going on outside. Finally the great day comes when

After several months a young kangaroo pokes its head out of the mother's pouch.

The baby koala rides on his mother's back until he is almost as big as she is.

it first ventures from its shelter. This may be as much as six months or more after its birth. The baby stays close to its mother and bounces right back into the protective pocket at the first sign of danger. In a few weeks it has outgrown the pouch and is ready to leave for good.

Another favorite marsupial is the Australian koala or Teddy bear. Unlike most of the other marsupials, it has a pouch opening to the rear. At birth the three-quarter-inch baby goes immediately into the pouch. By the time it is six months old, it is seven inches long and well covered with fur. After another two months it comes out of the pouch and clings to its mother's back. She carries the baby around until it is nearly as big as she is. Finally the little koala is weaned onto a diet of eucalyptus or gum leaves and leaves its mother for good.

The only pouched animal found in the United States is the Virginia opossum. Baby opossums are amazing little creatures, born after a gestation period of only twelve days. A mother may have as many as fifteen or twenty in a litter, each no bigger than a housefly. As soon as it is born, each tiny youngster starts a mad scramble for the pouch. Its journey is made easy by the path the mother has licked through her fur. As soon as it arrives in the pouch, each young one attaches itself to an available nipple. There are never more than thirteen nipples in the pouch, sometimes only eleven. If there are more young than nipples, the late arrivals starve to death.

The more fortunate ones develop rapidly. In a week they have increased their birth weight ten times. In nine weeks they are as big as full-grown mice.

Half-grown opossums leave their mother's pouch and cling to her back.

Then they can venture out of the pouch and cling to their mother's back. Like strap-hangers on a subway, they wrap their bare tails around their mother's tail as an aid in hanging on. By fall they are big enough to strike out on their own.

How Mammals Carry Their Young

Lots of mammals have young which are helpless at birth. They have to be carried from one place to another in an emergency. There are many reasons why the mother may move them. She may take them away from forest fires or floods or hide them from animals which threaten them. If they cannot keep up with her on her daily wanderings, she may carry them part of the time. The way in which she carries them depends on what kind of mammal she is.

Rodents, or gnawing animals, have a variety of methods. Baby rats and mice sometimes cling tightly to their mother's nipples and are dragged behind her as she flees from danger. This may not be a very efficient method of escape, for the mother is slowed down by the load, and the whole family may be captured at once. A female gray squirrel moves her young one at a time. She seizes the youngster by the soft stretchy skin on its belly. It then curls its body around either side of her head and is carried that way. Sometimes a beaver mother walks on her hind legs and carries her offspring in her outstretched arms. This is the way a human mother carries her baby except that the beaver mother has her hands open, palms downward. The outstretched arms merely serve as a platform for holding the baby.

Bats, the only true fliers among the mammals, have one or two young at a time. For the first few days after they are born, the young of many native bats are carried about with the mother on her nocturnal flights after insects. They cling to the fur of her belly as she swoops back and forth through the summer darkness. After they are a few days old, the mother bat leaves them back at the roost, hanging upside down when she goes out hunting.

The young of many bats are carried about by the mother for the first few days.

Shrews, those fierce, mouse-sized hunters, have an unusual way of getting their babies out of tight spots. Each baby grabs the rump of the next one. The mother retreats, pulling a chain of young behind her.

The meat-eaters, or carnivores, generally transport their young in their mouths. A cat will carry its kitten by the loose skin at the nape of its neck. A big cat, such as a lion or tiger, sometimes grasps its tiny cub about the body. Its huge teeth and great bone-crushing jaws close down with infinite gentleness on the squirming cub. Sometimes a mother black bear grasps her cub by the head and carries it that way. A female polar bear may carry her young on her back for long overland trips. If the baby polar bear gets tired in the water, it grabs its mother's stubby tail with its sharp teeth and lets her tow it for awhile.

Another aquatic mammal, the sea otter, floats on her back and holds her young one snugly against her breast with her forelegs. Cradled in its mother's arms, the baby otter nurses and sleeps, rocked by the motion of the waves. Manatees sometimes hold their young in similar fashion with their flippers while the baby nurses. Porpoises and whales will get under their newly born offspring and push them to the surface to get their first breath of air.

The young of that odd, toothless animal from South America, the giant anteater, sometimes rides on its mother's back, just forward of her tail.

Monkeys and great apes have several different methods for carrying their young. The baby frequently clings to its mother's abdomen, with its face close to her breasts. Those tiny South American monkeys, the marmosets, usually have twin babies which may hang onto their mother's back or drape

The young of the giant anteater sometimes rides on its mother's back.

themselves around her neck like a fur piece or around her hips. The father marmoset often relieves the mother and does his share of the baby-carrying.

Mother Love

Baby furred animals need more care for a longer period of time than the young of any other group of animals. They would die quickly if the parents did not feed and protect them.

The mother mammal starts to look out for her young as soon as it is born. First she plucks or licks away the birth membranes which may still be around it. Otherwise the baby might suffocate. As soon as the membranes are cleared away, the mother often licks the baby all over. This cleans the baby off and stimulates its circulation. Soon the baby is looking for its first meal. If it has to stand in order to nurse, the mother nuzzles it, encouraging it to get up. A baby calf or fawn will wobble and fall repeatedly before it finally stays up.

From the first day on, the mother nurses her baby, shelters it from rain and storm, protects it from danger, and helps it learn how to survive. Most mammal mothers fight fiercely to protect their young from harm. Any farm boy who has tampered with an old sow and her litter of piglets knows that. A female American buffalo or bison can be one of the fiercest animals when a meat-eater comes after her calf. Walrus mothers will even attack a boat when their young are threatened by hunters. Even timid small mammals may stand up to an enemy to protect their young from harm.

Like certain birds, some mammal mothers try to lure an enemy away from their offspring. The pronghorn antelope is one of these. The mother pronghorn usually has twins, which can run at the rate of twenty-five miles an hour, within a few days of their birth. That is speedy enough to outdistance most enemies. Until they are able to run, however, the mother hides each one under a different bush or patch of tumble-weed. Here the fawn curls up and becomes an almost invisible part of the landscape. The mother is never very far away. If a hungry wolf or coyote approaches, she runs close to the hunter, as though tempting him to chase her. If he follows, she bounds off, keeping just ahead of him, and leading him as far away from her young ones as she can. Then she puts on an effort-

The walrus mother is a fierce protector of her young.

less burst of speed which puts her far ahead of her pursuer.

Animals in captivity usually exhibit the same affection for their young as animals in the wild. Some-

A tiger mother carries her cub with great care.

times, however, the artificial surroundings of cage life may change the mother's natural feelings. If she does not get the privacy or quiet she needs for bearing and raising her young, she may abandon them or kill them.

Tigers seldom make good parents in captivity because of their nervous temperaments. Rajpur and Dacca, a pair of Bengal tigers at the New York Zoological Park, are exceptions. Raised by human beings from their infancy, these tigers are tame and affectionate. They have been the parents of nine litters of young—a total of twenty-nine cubs in all. Dacca has been a model mother.

This maternal instinct is so strong in mammals that a mother who has lost her own babies can often be induced to care for the young of other animals, even orphans of an entirely different species. The foster mothers nurse and care for these youngsters as though they were their own. This can happen with animals that are natural enemies in the wild.

Every year the newspapers carry stories and pictures showing a mother cat raising a baby rabbit or squirrel, along with her own litter. A cat may also accept puppies and a mother dog will often accept kittens. Sentimental circus people tell the story of a tiny mongrel dog that was given an orphan lion cub to nurse. As the cub grew, a strong bond formed between it and its foster mother. Even when the cub had grown into a magnificent big maned lion, a star of the Big Top, it still showed affection for the little dog one-twentieth its size.

Family Life Among the Monkeys

Practically all kinds of monkeys and apes travel in bands or family groups. The dominant males lead the band and guard it against danger. They usually ignore the young, which are cared for by the females. Each baby monkey stays close to its mother until it is old enough to crawl about and start eating solid foods. As it grows, it gains in strength and confidence. Soon it is playing with other youngsters in the band. They wrestle and fight and play leapfrog. They tease one another and play tricks on their elders. They are full of curiosity and have to investigate everything. In short, they get into lots of mischief.

Sometimes the males of the band will discipline the young whether they need it or not. This happened in a family of Guinea baboons at the zoo. Father baboon usually sat by himself in regal dignity, unmindful of the antics of his eldest son. Junior was quite a tease. Sometimes he would run up and tweak his father's ear playfully or leap over him. If Papa happened to be in a good mood, he would ignore this monkey business. If he was grouchy for any reason, though, he was apt to turn and give the high-spirited youngster a good hiding. Then Junior would stay away from his irate parent until the next time.

As with other animals, captivity may radically change the feelings a mother monkey has for her young, or the baby's feelings for others of its own kind. I remember the case of a baby wanderoo monkey, or lion-tailed macaque, from India. He was the first offspring of a gentle young mother who had been captured when very young and raised in captivity. From her actions, she obviously did not know what to do about the strange little creature to which she had given birth. She had no mother around, no aunts or kinfolk of any sort, to set an example for her. So, not knowing what to do, she left the baby lying on the floor of the cage. In order to save its life, the youngster was removed to the zoo's hospital. Here it was raised on the bottle, and grew up to be the

Baby Uele colobus monkeys are entirely white at birth.

spoiled pet of everyone on the staff. The little monkey was perfectly at home with human beings—but not with monkeys.

Another type of behavior is shown in the case of the first baby Uele colobus monkey ever born in captivity. This, too, happened in the Bronx Zoo. Uele colobus monkeys come from Central Africa and are very beautiful. The adults have smooth, glistening, black fur with a fringe of long white hair on their backs. However, colobus babies have short, wavy coats that are entirely white at birth. At the Bronx Zoo a Uele colobus baby was born to one of two females that had been living with a male in perfect friendship ever since their capture as youngsters some years before. When the baby was born, the spinster female started a fierce struggle with the real mother for the possession of the baby. She had to be separated from the group to prevent her from tearing the baby limb from limb in her effort to take it from its rightful mother.

The great apes—gorillas, chimpanzees, orang-utans and gibbons—are similar to their smaller relatives in general family life and responsibilities. They have no fixed homes, but usually travel through the forests in small bands or family groups. They keep within a limited area and go where food is most plentiful. Each evening at sundown they bed down for sleep. Chimpanzees and orang-utans build strong sleeping platforms or nests of boughs in the trees. Sometimes female gorillas and their young do the same. But a big male gorilla, weighing four hundred pounds or more, is too heavy to risk tree branches at night. He makes his bed at the base of the trunk where he is ready to protect his family. In many ways gorillas are the most advanced of the great apes, but chimpanzees are generally more adaptable and easily trained.

A generation ago keeping gorillas alive in captivity was considered to be almost impossible. Even with good diet and care young ones died after a few weeks or months. The one exception was a baby gorilla, Johnny Daniel, that was brought to England in 1918 and raised in a private home. The little gorilla got all the care a human baby would get. He flourished as long as he received love and companionship along with proper diet and care. Once zoo men understood this need for affection, they were successful in keeping their gorillas healthy. However, no gorillas were ever born in captivity until 1956.

White-handed gibbons often travel in family groups.

All About Animals and Their Young

It happened in the zoo of Columbus, Ohio, where a pair of young adult gorillas, Baron and Christine, were prize possessions. These two had been brought up together from babyhood, getting all the care that human babies get. One morning when the keeper approached Christine's cage, he noticed something strange lying on the floor. It was a newborn gorilla. The inexperienced young mother was sitting on her shelf blinking uncertainly at the youngster, which looked dead. Obviously she did not know what to do about it.

Quickly the keeper shifted Christine into an adjoining enclosure and entered her cage. The baby stirred feebly. At least it was alive. The keeper stimulated the little animal's breathing by blowing into its mouth. Then he notified the zoo director, and the baby gorilla was placed in an improvised incubator. Doctors were called, and by the next day news of the baby had flashed around the world. Baron and Christine were the parents of the first gorilla ever born in captivity. The infant was soon named Colo, short for Columbus. With all the care and knowledge of modern medicine, nurses around the clock and frequent checking by baby specialists, Colo has grown and flourished.

If all goes well, she may have young of her own some-day. Modern zoos are learning more all the time about keeping and breeding all sorts of wild animals in captivity.

They're on Their Own!

Before a young mammal is ready to face the harsh realities of the outside world by itself, it has many things to learn. Some it learns by trial and error. Other things it learns by imitation. There are often many specific things that it learns from its mother. The problems and dangers which each type of mammal faces are different, so the education of each type of mammal differs too.

Many of the small mammals, like rats and mice, mature very fast. Their mother nurses and protects them as long as they need it, but they very quickly learn how to eat solid foods and how to escape from danger. These are the principal things they must know in order to survive. Fear and flight are practically instinctive with them.

Among higher mammals, training of the young is often a much longer and more complicated affair. The baby has to learn what foods are good and what are to be avoided. It may have to learn how to find special kinds of food. This may take long practice and constant imitation of the parent, especially if live prey has to be captured. If the animal spends part of its time in the water, as is the case with otters, the baby has to learn how to swim. Few baby mammals can swim instinctively. Most of them have to learn by practice. The mother supervises this, usually in shallow water, or in a place where she can help the youngster if it has trouble. The youngster must learn how to avoid dangers. It must know what it can expect from other kinds of animals, what it can expect from its own kind. It needs to know the customs and taboos of its own tribe.

The mother otter supervises her youngsters' swimming.

The young mammal absorbs a great many of these things by observing its elders and copying their behavior. Other things, like how and where to migrate or how to build a certain type of burrow or nest, seem to be instinctive—at least in part. Many things are learned directly from the mother. Before everything else, the baby must learn to do what its mother indicates and do it right away.

One of the best of all mammal mothers is the black bear. Her cubs have a great deal to learn in preparation for adult life, and the mother bear takes her duties seriously. The cubs are born in January or February while the old bear is hibernating in her winter den. The young are no bigger than kittens and are blind and helpless at birth. They snuggle against their mother, nursing and sleeping for many weeks. It will be several months before they even see the outside world.

At last, on some mild day in early spring, the mother bear ventures out of her den, followed by the cubs. By now they are covered with thick, fuzzy fur and are bright-eyed and alert. Everything in the outside world is new to them, and they set out to investigate it all. They roll on the ground and scratch at tree trunks. They smell and sniff at every plant, cuff the dried leaves and sample everything that might be edible. Their mother watches indulgently but keeps the cubs away from anything she thinks might cause trouble—such as a porcupine or a snake.

Every day the cubs learn something that adds to their knowledge. Their mother is a stern disciplinarian, and if danger threatens, she sends the cubs scooting up a tree with a warning grunt. They must not come down until she gives them the signal. Like many other animal mothers, a mother bear has a whole language of her own in which she communicates with her cubs.

By late summer she has weaned the youngsters and has introduced them to the delights of such tidbits as huckleberries, blackberries, wild honey, field mice, frogs, insect grubs, beechnuts and acorns. The cubs stay with their mother through that fall and usually through the winter. When they do strike out on their own the next summer, they go forth well prepared.

Observing Animals and Their Young at Home

You can learn a great deal about animals and their young by keeping a few of them at home and observ-

The mother bear tries to keep her cubs out of trouble.

ing their activities. Lots of small animals can be kept even in city apartments and will carry on their family life where you can watch them easily.

Tropical fish, for example, will flourish and breed even in small aquariums. You should have a second tank for the nursery. Otherwise some parent fish are likely to gulp down their own offspring in the limited space of their own tank. If you would rather keep native specimens, you can stock your aquarium with snails, tadpoles, newts and water insects from the nearest pond. A few frog or toad eggs can be gathered in the spring, and you can watch the development from egg to tadpole to toad.

A terrarium is fun to keep, too. This can be made easily by planting moss, ferns and other woodland plants in a glass tank. With the addition of moisture and a glass cover to keep the humidity constant, you can reproduce a small section of the forest. Tiny frogs and salamanders, as well as land snails, earthworms, and some insects, can be kept in the terrarium. Remember that most terrarium animals are insect eaters and prefer live food.

You may find it interesting to rear butterflies and moths, too. All the different stages of their life history,

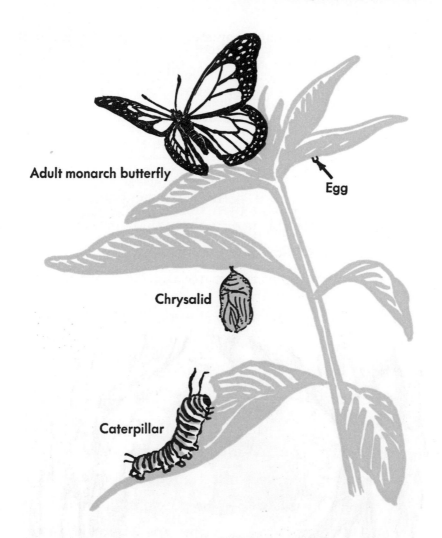

Adult monarch butterfly

Egg

Chrysalid

Caterpillar

from egg to adult, can be watched if you supply the caterpillars with the right plant food.

If you like birds, you can easily keep a canary or parakeet. Under the right conditions, either of these will raise young in captivity.

Among the mammals, hamsters and white mice can be kept indoors and will rear families if given half a chance. Domesticated birds and mammals like these usually make more satisfactory pets than their wild relatives. For one thing, it is against the law in many states to keep most wild birds and mammals in captivity without a special permit. In the great majority of cases they would not make good pets anyway. While they are babies, they may be cunning and tame. However, they often revert to the wild when they

Usually the timid wood mouse does not make a good pet.

138

grow up. Wood mice breed readily in captivity, but are too shy to make good pets.

Nine times out of ten, when people come across a baby wild bird or mammal without its mother, they decide that the youngster has been abandoned. They pick up the little wild creature and carry it home to be raised as a pet. Usually the mother animal has not abandoned her young at all but has merely left it for a short time.

The only time to pick up a baby wild bird or mammal is when it is injured or you are sure the parents are dead or have abandoned it. In cases like these, nestlings can be kept temporarily in an improvised nest in a box lined with dried grass or soft torn-up paper. The little birds need to be kept warm, clean and dry. Most important of all, they need to be fed at frequent intervals all day long. A satisfactory basic food for most songbirds can be made by mixing crumbled zwieback or crackers with grated carrot and the yolk of hard-boiled egg. A few drops of water may be added to make the mixture moist and crumbly, but not wet. Then it can be rolled into soft balls or picked up in tweezers, and the baby birds gulp it down hungrily. Insects and bits of earthworm are also

A motherless baby chipmunk can be given milk with a dropper.

taken readily, as are pieces of soft fruit such as mealy apple, grape and cherry.

An even, warm temperature and clean, dry surroundings are important for baby mammals too. Baby rabbits and squirrels can be placed in an improvised nest like that used for baby birds. They also need to be fed frequently throughout the day. Depending on their size, they can be given milk from a doll's nursing bottle, from a medicine dropper or even from a spoon. Some babies are slow to get the idea of nursing, but they will learn if you keep trying. A good formula is equal parts of cow's milk and water heated to body temperature. If it seems to agree with the baby, try it with less water. Some babies take full-strength milk from the beginning.

Each day the little mammals may be offered bits of their natural food. Young squirrels and rabbits often begin to eat greens, vegetables or other solid foods long before you think they should, for they develop very quickly. Pablum and cod-liver oil can soon be added to the milk. Gradually, as they eat more solids, the babies can be weaned. Then, just as their animal parents would, you can teach them how to find their own food. The day will soon come when they can take care of themselves, and you can let them go.

Index

Index

Index

Index

allabout
books